crazy sexy asian

sexy

/ Sɛksi /

Learn how to pronounce

adjective

    1. 1 .

    sexually attractive or exciting.

    "sexy French underwear"

synonyms:

sexually attractive, seductive , desirable , alluring , inviting ,
sensual , sultry , slinky , provocative , tempting , tantalizing ;
More
nubile , voluptuous , shapely , luscious , lush ;
feline ;
bedroom ;
flirtatious , coquettish ;
informal hot , fanciable , beddable , come-hither , come-to-bed
;
informal fit , mortgage ;
informal foxy , cute , bootylicious;
informal spunky ;
vulgar slang fuck me
"she's so sexy"
erotic , arousing, exciting , stimulating , hot ;
sexually explicit, titillating , suggestive , racy , risqué ,
provocative , spicy , juicy , adult, X-rated ;
ore , coarse , smutty , pornographic , vulgar , crude , lewd ,
lubricious ;
informal raunchy , steamy , naughty , horny , porn , blue , skin ;
informal saucy , fruity ;
informal gamy
"a TV show featuring sexy home videos"

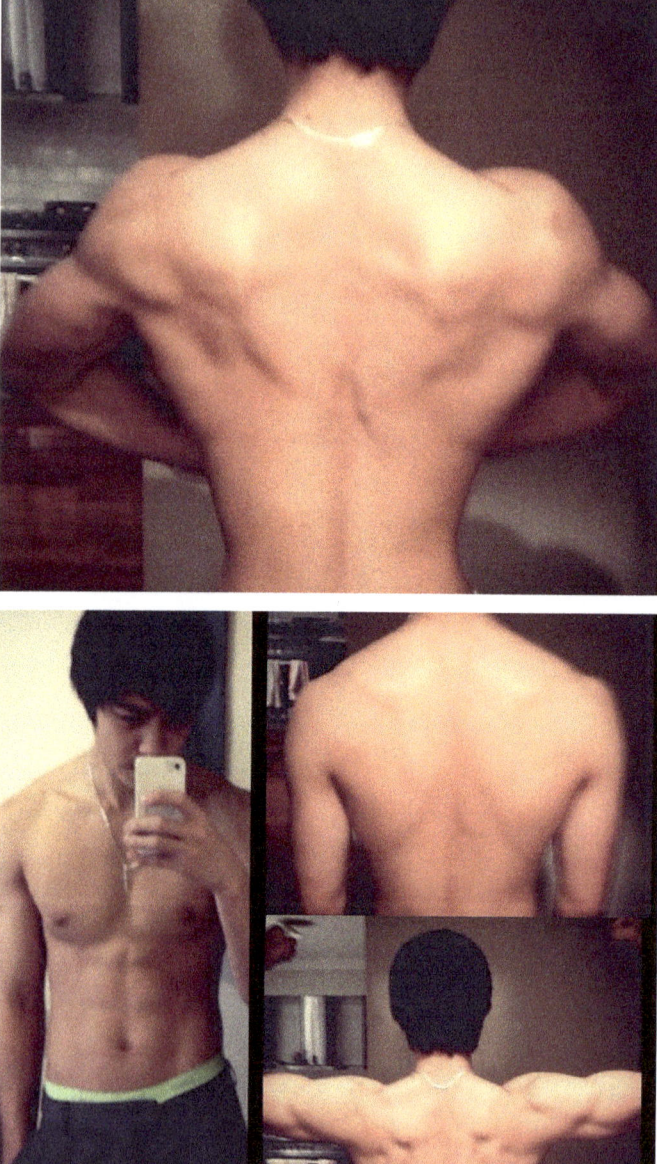

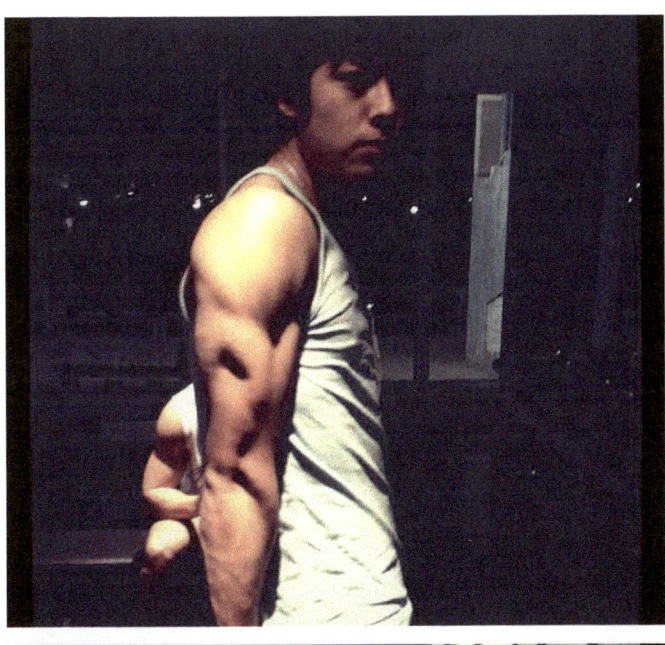

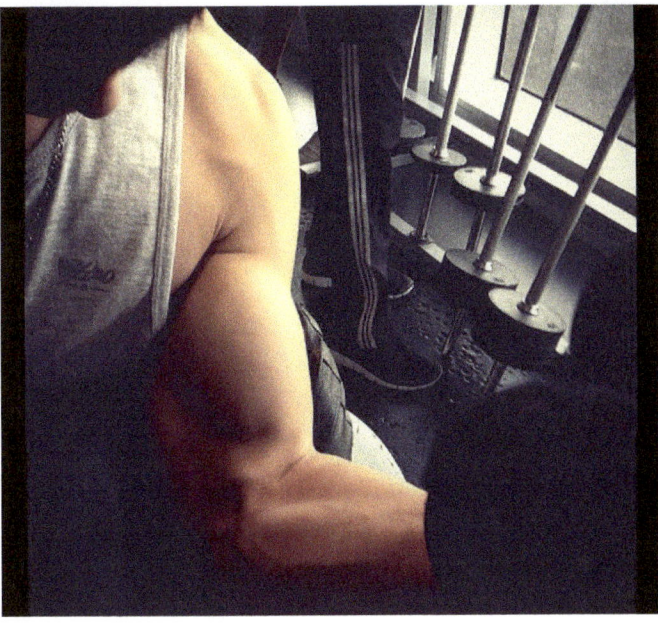

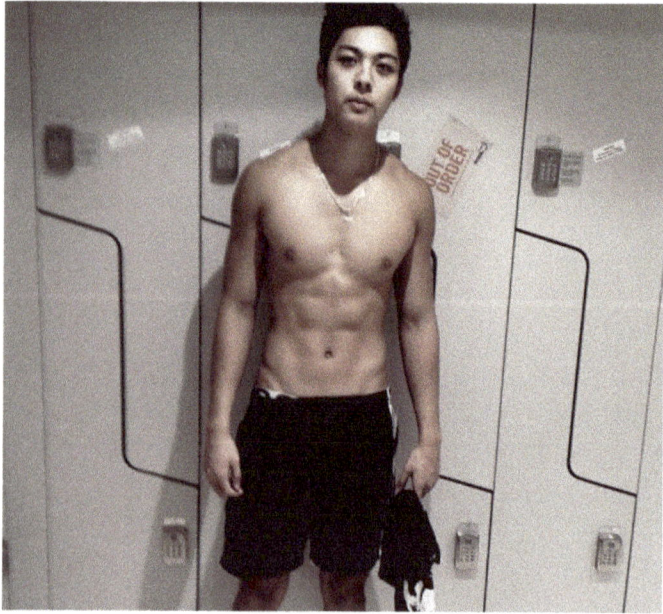

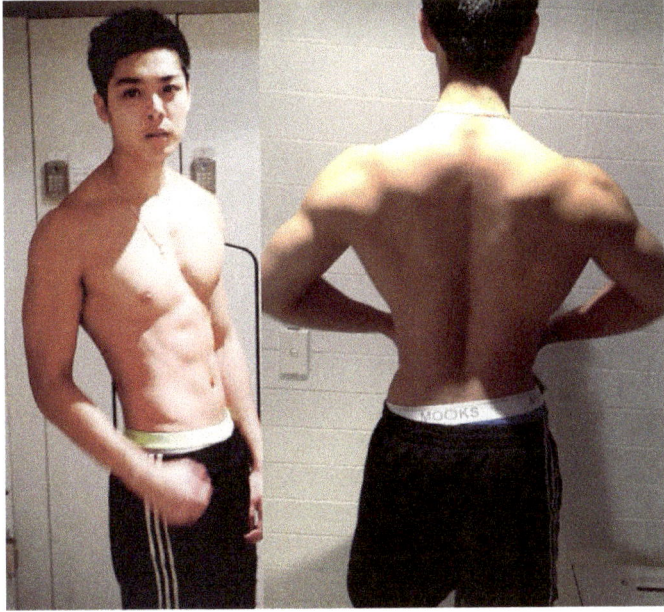

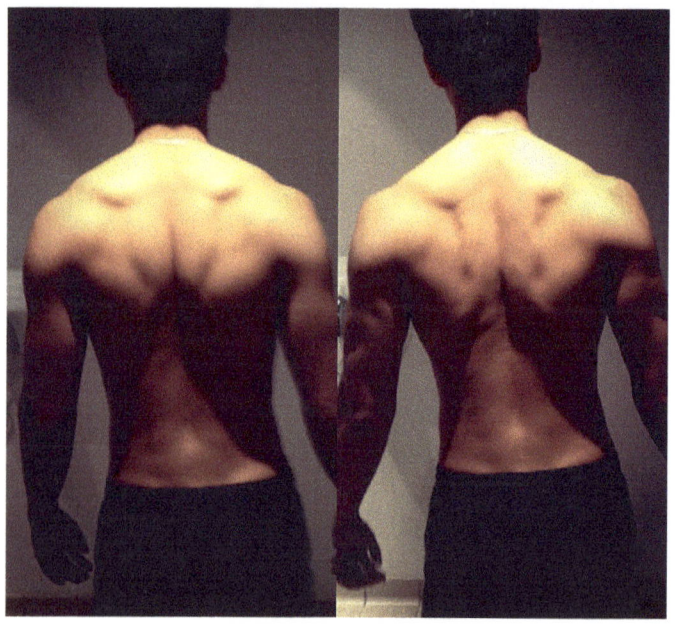

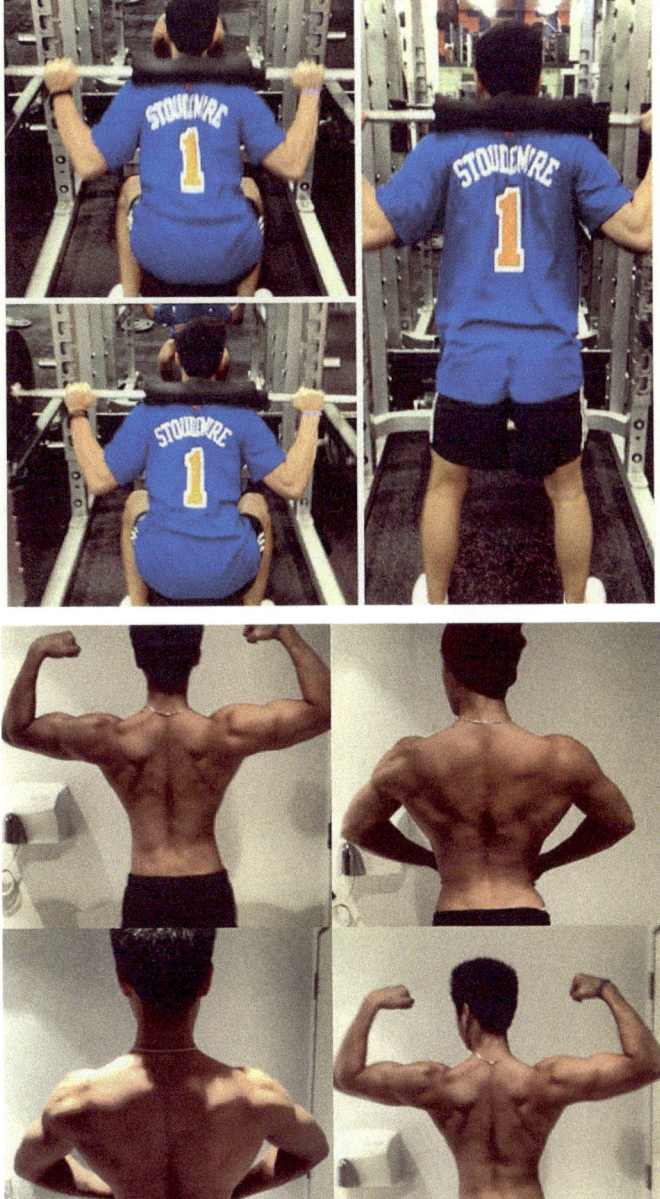

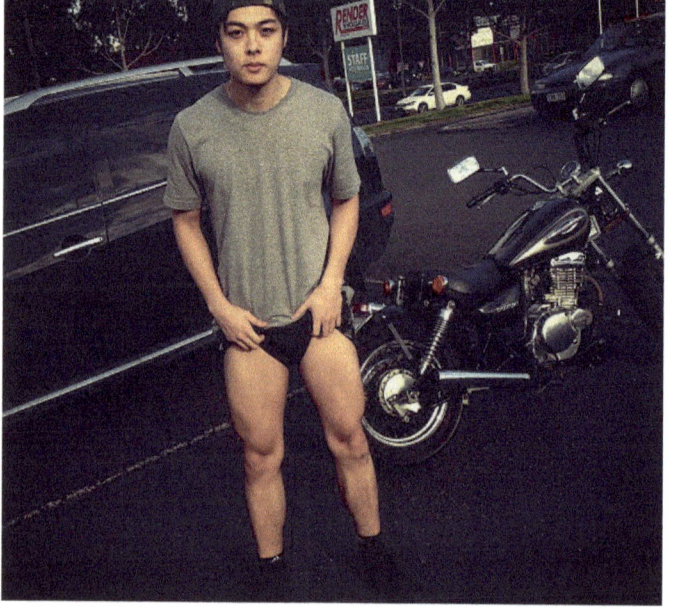

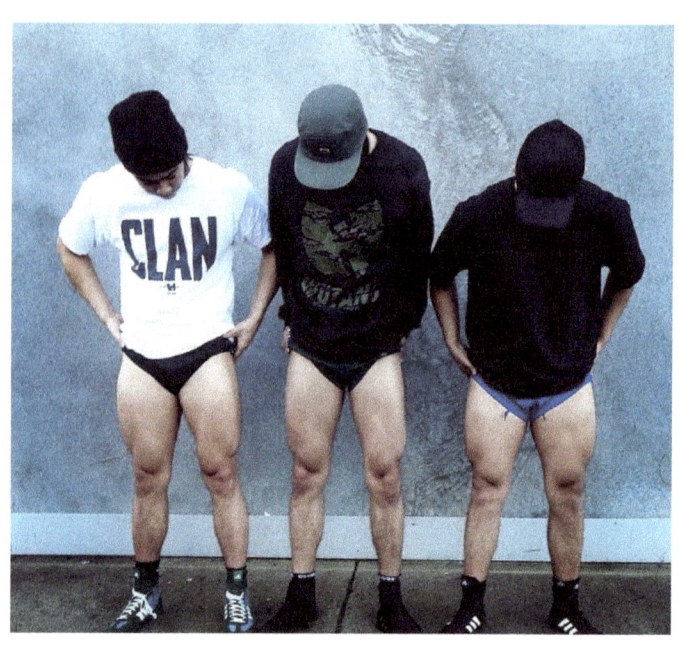

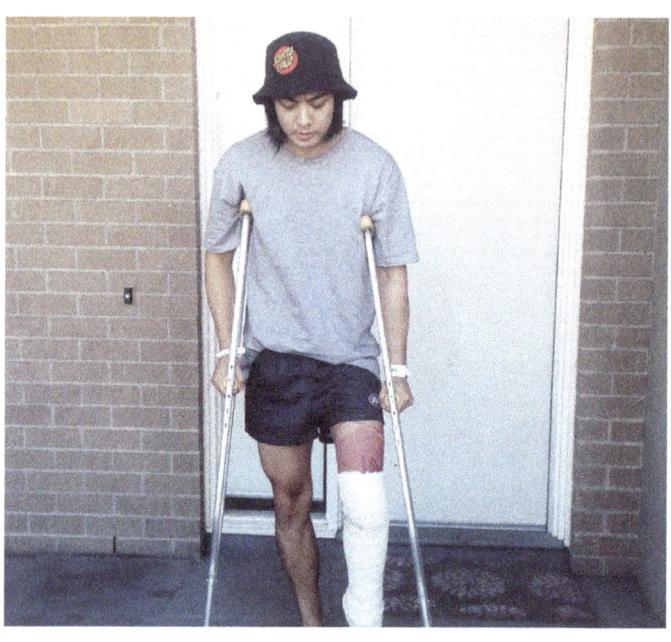

TREE WORKS
IN
PROGRESS
DO NOT

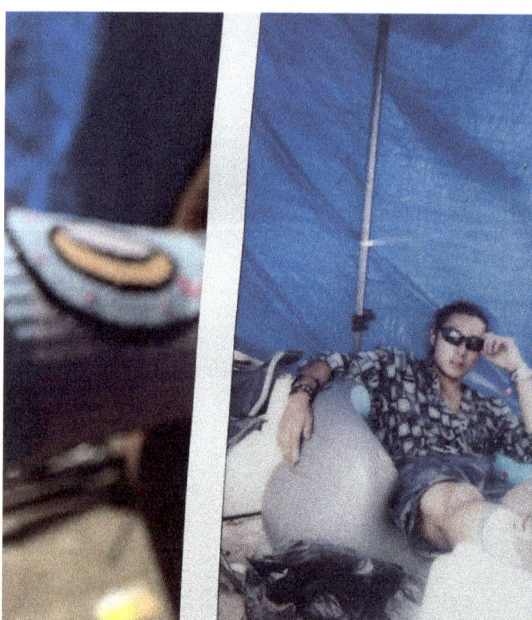

CPSIA information can be obtained
at www.ICGtesting.com
Printed in the USA
BVHW022013280719
554531BV00011B/422/P